"Life imitates Art far more than

Art imitates Life."

- Oscar Wilde
(Written in 1889, not sure he would agree today)

TATTOOS & POETRY

A.G. SULLIVAN

Tattoos & Poetry

ISBN: 978-1-7342443-6-6
Library of Congress Control Number: xxx

First Edition: August 2024

DISCLAIMER

S2 publishing group

www.agsullivan.info

CONTENTS

BOOKS BY A.G. SULLIVAN

The Katzenstein Kids and the Eye of Horus
The Katzenstein Kids and the 12 Minotaurs
Trypophobia – A Novel

If you enjoyed this book, also available is the companion
Journal: **Tattoos & Poetry Journal**

Available on Amazon

POEMS OF RESILIENCE AND REBIRTH!

In this collection of 65 raw and evocative poems, we explore the intricate tapestry of lives touched by adversity. Each verse delves into the depths of human experience, illuminating the strength and resilience found in the face of love, abuse, mental disorder, cancer, addiction, recovery, and identity.

Through poignant words, we honor the scars that tell stories of battles fought and won. We celebrate the courage of those who have dared to rise above their circumstances, embracing their journey with unwavering spirit.

Poems that touch on life and its incredible journey, with moments of joy, resilience, serenity, and profound human connection. Our individual adventure, as we celebrate and honor the precious gift of existence and the beauty of the world around us.

ART IMITATING LIFE!

The challenges we face and the experiences we cherish are often deeply personal, etching themselves into our very being. In the world of art and expression, tattoos offer a unique and powerful way to individualize these moments, transforming them into wearable symbols of our journey through life. Each tattoo tells a story, a visual representation of our triumphs, struggles, and the lessons learned along the way.

The artistry of tattooing allows us to capture the essence of our experiences in intricate designs, colors, and symbols that hold deep meaning. A single image can encapsulate a lifetime of memories, emotions, personal growth, and our individuality. These tattoos become a part of us, a permanent reminder of the challenges we've overcome, the love we've shared, the loss we've endured, and the resilience we've discovered within ourselves.

LOVE

SOULS UNITE

In dreams, where eyelids close and visions start,
I journey to a world, a sacred, hidden part.
Beyond the cosmic dance of moon and star,
Lies a haven, untouched, where only we are.

Just you and I, in this realm serene,
Where love's pure light forever gleams.
Underneath the moon's soft, silvery glow,
Our souls entwine, and passions overflow.

We touch, we cling, with hearts aflame,
Embracing love, a never-ending game.
In this dreamscape, you're my cherished wife,
A perfect life, free from worldly strife.

Our souls unite, a touch both deep and true,
Each whispered word, a bond forever new.
My love, my partner, through all life's design,
Will you be mine, in this world and time?

You & Me

LOVE'S SONG

Heart beats like a drum,
Two souls entwined as one dance,
Love's song fills the air.

CRESENT LIGHT

The sun hangs low, a crescent light,
The nights stretch long, devoid of delight.
Since you departed, my dearest love,
A chasm yawns, a void above.

The world, once vibrant, feels empty and gray,
No shared laughter, no words to convey.
The joys we cherished, the moments so sweet,
Now echo hollow, incomplete.

I yearn for your touch, a gentle caress,
Your scent, your voice, a lingering trace.
The jokes we shared, the smiles we exchanged,
A love so profound, a bond unchained.

Partner, lover, best friend, and more,
The void you left, forever sore.
Yet hope remains, a flicker so bright,
In a realm of peace, bathed in celestial light.

Until that day, when we'll meet once more,
Beyond this pain, on a far distant shore,
I'll hold you close, within my heart's embrace,
In memories cherished, a sacred space.

LUMINOUS WARMTH

Luminous warmth that fills my heart,
Overwhelming joy, right from the start.
Vibrant colors painted in the sky,
Everlasting bond that will never die.
Though tears may flow, and hearts may ache,
Know that my love, no death can take.

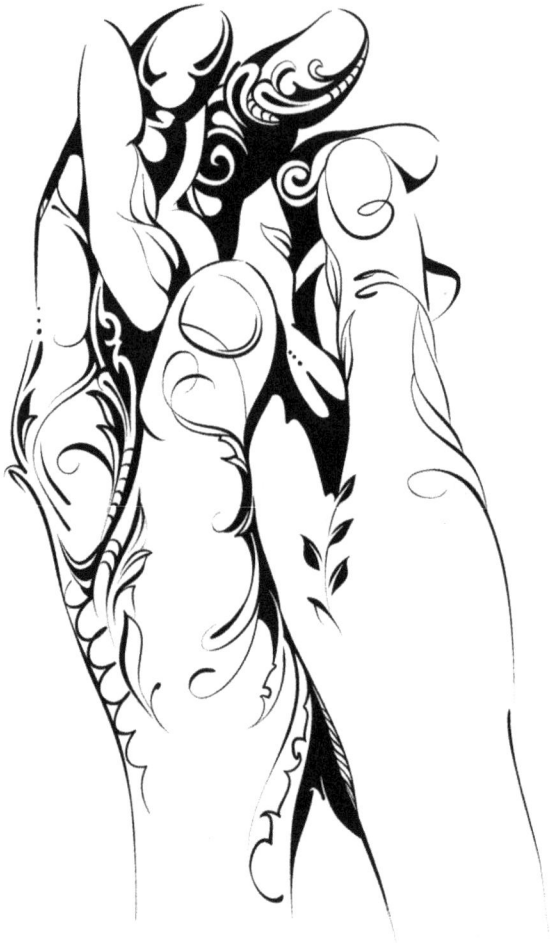

A MISSED CHANCE

In fields of memory, where shadows play,
A figure lingers, from a distant day.
The one who got away, a fleeting glance,
A love unspoken, a missed chance.

A lifetime's journey, with paths untrod,
Yet in my heart, a garden's fertile sod.
For seeds were sown, in moments shared so brief,
A love that bloomed, beyond belief.

The years may pass, like petals in the breeze,
But roots run deep, beneath the swaying trees.
A tender shoot, a memory's embrace,
A love that lingers, in time and space.

Perhaps the seed, they planted long ago,
Was meant to grow, a love we'll never know.
A silent promise, a whispered vow,
A garden tended, forever now.

So let it bloom, this love that never died,
A testament to dreams, that sleep inside.
For in the heart, where memories reside,
The one who got away, forever abides.

A FATHER'S LOVE

In your strong arms, I found my safe haven,
A father's love, a gift from heaven.
Your strength a fortress, protecting me,
A gentle giant, for all to see.

With understanding eyes, you saw my soul,
Guiding me through life, making me whole.
In every challenge, your wisdom shone,
A steady hand, a love I've known.

Your laughter echoed, a joyful sound,
Filling my world, with love unbound.
A princess in your eyes, a precious pearl,
You made me feel cherished, your little girl.

In every lesson, a tender heart,
You taught me how love should impart.
Respect and kindness, a man's true worth,
A legacy carried, for all it's worth.

With every hug, and every gentle kiss,
You showed me love's purest bliss.
A father's bond, a love so deep,
A treasure I'll forever keep.

For in your heart, I found my place,
A daughter's love, forever embraced.
My hero, my teacher, my guiding light,
Thank you, dear father, for making life bright.

FIELDS OF GOLD

In fields of gold, where sunlight gently gleams,
I found a love that set my soul alight.
Your eyes, like stars, ignited tender dreams,
And filled my heart with warmth, both day and night.

Your touch, a symphony of sweet delight,
Sent shivers through my veins, a gentle fire.
Your smile, a beacon, radiant and bright,
A guiding light, my heart's one true desire.

With every word, you paint a world anew,
A tapestry of joy, where love takes flight.
In every glance, I find a love so true,
A bond unyielding, shining ever bright.

So let our hearts entwine, forevermore,
In this sweet dance of love, forever yours.

ABUSE

RESILIENCE

In shadows dwelling, where love turned cold,
A woman weeps, her spirit controlled.
Bruised body trembles, eyes filled with fright,
A captive heart, yearning for the light.

His words like daggers, piercing her soul,
Crushing her spirit, taking their toll.
Broken promises whispered in the night,
Stealing her joy, extinguishing her light.

Yet deep within, a flicker remains,
A mother's love, defying the chains.
For tiny hands reach, seeking her embrace,
Innocent eyes mirroring her pain.

With trembling heart, she makes a choice,
To rise above the deafening noise.
For her children's sake, she'll find her might,
Breaking free from the endless night.

Though fear may linger, her spirit takes flight,
A wounded warrior, stepping into the light.
With each faltering step, her strength renewed,
She'll shield her children, as mothers do.

No longer bound by shackles unseen,
She reclaims her power, forever serene.
In the tapestry of resilience, she weaves,
A testament to love that never leaves.

TINY DANCER

Beneath the glare, her body gleams,
A dancer's smile, a façade it seems.
Her eyes betray a hidden pain,
A yearning soul, a life in vain.

A doctor's coat, a lawyer's might,
A teacher's wisdom, her true delight.
But dreams are costly, ambitions bold,
So on she dances, for coins of gold.

For men who watch, their eyes aflame,
She moves with grace, a gilded frame.
Yet in each step, a silent plea,
A dance for hope, for destiny.

One day she'll rise, her spirit free,
Leaving this stage, her legacy.
To halls of learning, she will ascend,
A future bright, her life to mend.

No more tiny dancer, bound by fate,
A new path chosen, a life to create.
But until then, the music plays,
She'll dance tonight, for brighter days.

INNOCENCE SOLD

In shadowed room, where hope takes flight,
A girl prepares, to face the night.
Her body trembles, her soul feels numb,
As desperation whispers, "Just succumb."

The weight of need, a heavy crown,
A bitter bargain, for a few bills down.
Her innocence sold, a sacrifice made,
A silent scream, a soul betrayed.

The man approaches, his eyes alight,
With lustful hunger, devoid of right.
She closes her eyes, a silent plea,
To numb the pain, the misery.

Through gritted teeth, she endures the shame,
A puppet dancing, in a cruel game.
Her body a vessel, a hollow shell,
A price to pay, for a living hell.

Each touch a violation, a searing brand,
On a heart that yearns for a different hand.
A stolen moment, a fleeting gain,
A broken spirit, etched in pain.

But in the depths of her despair, a spark,
A flicker of defiance, piercing the dark.
She'll rise above this, one day soon,
And find her freedom, beneath the moon.

For though her body may be sold for gold,
Her spirit remains, untamed and bold.
A survivor's fire, a burning flame,
She'll find her power, reclaim her name.

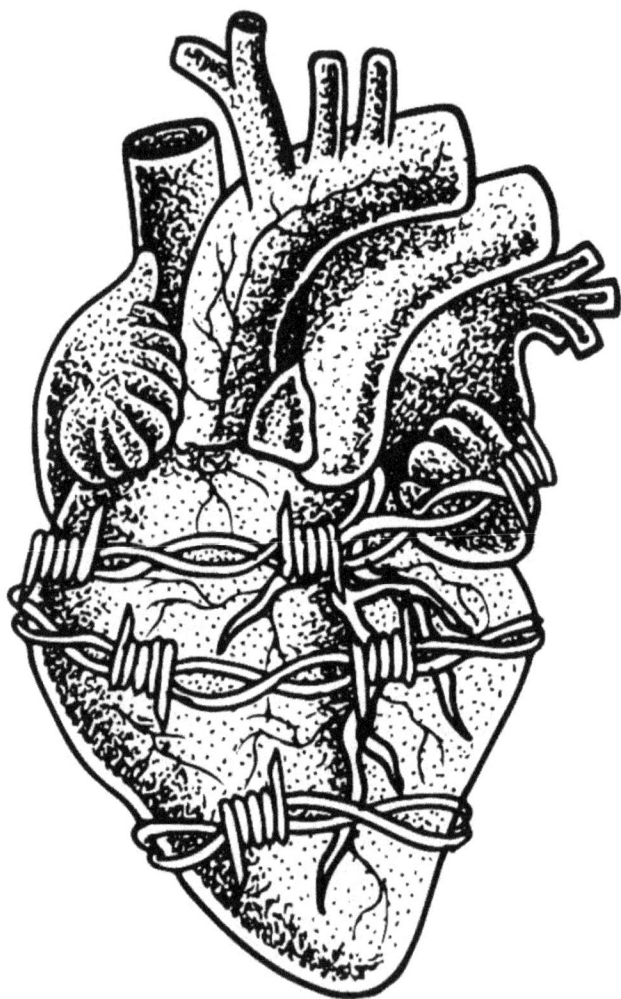

TWISTED LOVE

In twisted love, a tender heart was bound,
By cruel hands that sought to break and bruise.
In whispered threats, a spirit was unsound,
By words that cut like blades, and sharp abuse.

The tender touch that once brought sweet delight,
Became a weapon wielded in the night.
The gentle kiss, a memory now defiled,
By lips that twisted love, so meek and mild.

The scars unseen, yet etched upon the soul,
A silent scream that echoes, taking toll.
The shattered trust, a mirror cracked in two,
Reflecting pain, where love once grew.

But courage rises, from the ashes deep,
To break the silence, and the secrets keep.

PLUCKED PETALS

In innocence, I bloomed, a fragile flower,
Each petal soft, held love's sacred power.
With open heart, I offered it to those,
Who swore devotion, whispered tender prose.

But thorns concealed, beneath their velvet touch,
False promises unfurled, betraying much.
They plucked my petals, with deceitful art,
And left me bruised, a wounded, broken heart.

Each whispered word, a poisoned, cruel dart,
Inflicting pain, that tore my soul apart.
I felt their greed, their selfish, dark desire,
They sought to conquer, fueled by lustful fire.

In darkness veiled, I sought solace in vain,
As echoes of violation, left their stain.
Yet deep within, a flicker still remained,
A hope for love, a solace to be gained.

For though I've fallen, time and time again,
I'll rise once more, from ashes, born anew.
With resilience forged, and spirit untamed,
I'll find a love, that heals my wounds, unnamed.

And when that day arrives, in radiant light,
The scars will fade, and darkness take its flight.
For love's embrace, shall mend my shattered soul,
And banish shadows, making me whole.

CRUEL WORDS

The echo of his voice, a haunting refrain,
Each syllable a barb, inflicting pain.
Words that cut like glass, slicing through her soul,
Deeper than any blade, taking their toll.

His fists may bruise, leaving marks that fade,
But cruel words linger, a venomous parade.
Each insult a poison, seeping through her veins,
Leaving scars unseen, a lifetime of stains.

In the hollow of his gaze, she sees her worth,
Diminished, broken, trampled in the dirt.
His words a weapon, wielded with cruel intent,
Shattering her spirit, leaving her spent.

Yet in the quiet moments, when he's not around,
A flicker of defiance, a strength profound.
For though his words may wound, they cannot erase,
The essence of her being, her inner grace.

In the tapestry of pain, hope finds a thread,
A whisper of resilience, softly spread.
For she knows deep within, though battered and bruised,
Her spirit will endure, forever infused.

With the courage to rise, she'll break the chains,
And find her voice again, amidst the rains.
For words may wound, but they cannot destroy,
The fire within her, the source of her joy.

SILENT SCREAMS

Silent screams unheard,
Bruises fade, pain lingers on,
Love's twisted shadow.

LOVE BETRAYED

In a shattered trust, a love betrayed,
A partner's vows, so carelessly swayed.
They sought comfort in another's embrace,
Unraveling the threads of love's gentle lace.

Their partner's heart, a fragile bloom,
Now wilting in sorrow's consuming gloom.
Each whispered secret, a piercing dart,
Shattering their world, tearing it apart.

The bed they shared, now cold and wide,
Haunted by shadows, where love once lied.
They toss and turn, with tear-stained eyes,
As memories fade, and trust dies.

In the mirror's reflection, a stranger's gaze,
A broken partner, lost in a maze.
Should they forgive, and try to rebuild,
Or walk away, leaving love unfulfilled?

The battle rages, within their soul,
Between forgiveness and letting go.
The pain so deep, it leaves them numb,
As they struggle to find a way to overcome.

The weight of betrayal, a heavy load,
Crushing their spirit, a long and winding road.
But amidst the wreckage, a flicker of light,
A glimmer of hope, for a future bright.

With time as their ally, can they mend and heal,
And rediscover the love they once did feel.
Whether they chooses to stay or to part,
They'll find their strength, a brand new start.

A SWAN REBORN

In shadows cast, I waddled, awkward grace,
An ugly duckling, in a lonely chase.
With feathers ruffled, and a spirit dimmed,
I sought a stage, where I could be redeemed.

And then I rose, upon a gilded pole,
A swan emerging, shedding old control.
With every spin, a transformation bold,
I found my rhythm, as my story was told.

In swirling lights, my body learned to fly,
A graceful dance, beneath the hungry eye.
Each movement, a poem, etched in flesh and bone,
A silent language, meant for me alone.

They saw desire, in my every twist and turn,
A siren's call, to which their hearts would yearn.
But I saw freedom, in their eager gaze,
A power claimed, in this seductive maze.

For in that space, where shadows danced and swayed,
The ugly duckling, finally found its way.
I danced for me, with passion pure and bright,
A swan reborn, in the shimmering light.

So let them watch, with eyes that yearn and crave,
I'll dance my dance, and let their souls be saved.
For in this art, a beauty I've unfurled,
The ugly duckling, soaring in the world.

DISORDER

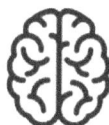

DEVOURED

In vibrant hues, a serpent's tail did glide,
Across the path where contentment did preside.
Complacent heart, with dreams fulfilled and bright,
Lured by the serpent's scales, a dazzling sight.

Blue skies above, and trees reaching high,
Forgotten now, as curiosity did fly.
The path once walked, with purpose and with grace,
Abandoned for the serpent's alluring chase.

Through tangled woods, the shimmering trail did lead,
To where a mighty snake did rear its head.
Its jaws agape, a captured deer within,
Struggling for life, amidst the serpent's din.

In wonder and awe, the spectacle I sought,
A masterpiece of nature, strangely wrought.
The deer's despair, a fleeting, poignant sight,
As freedom's spark ignited in its flight.

A glance exchanged, between the deer and me,
As it escaped the serpent's grasp, so suddenly.
But joy turned fear, as the serpent's gaze did turn,
Distracted by its beauty, a lesson to learn.

Smaller than the deer, with nowhere left to hide,
Fear gripped my heart, as fate did coincide.
Hopes and dreams, once held so very dear,
Lost in the woods, consumed by growing fear.

The serpent's maw, a gaping, hungry void,
Lessons unlearned, connections destroyed.
No more dreams, no more thrills, no more delight,
Devoured by the darkness, lost in endless night.

EVERY CUT

In rooms of quiet desperation,
Where shadows dance and whispers creep,
She finds solace in crimson creation,
A canvas of pain, a wound so deep.

Each silver line, a silent confession,
A testament to a soul's unrest,
A desperate plea for self-possession,
In wounds that mirror a heart suppressed.

With trembling hand and blade so keen,
She etches her story upon her skin,
A symphony of anguish, unseen,
A battle fought where shadows begin.

Each drop of blood, a bittersweet tear,
A testament to the void within,
A desperate grasp for what is near,
A fragile dance where scars begin.

In every cut, a silent scream,
A desperate plea to be heard,
A fight for life, a fleeting dream,
A fragile hope, a whispered word.

Never Give Up

INVISIBLE WOUNDS

Mind adrift in swirling tides,
Emotions tangled, hidden inside.
Numbness steals away the light,
Trapped in shadows, day and night.
Alone, but longing for connection,
Lost in labyrinths of introspection.
Invisible wounds that ache and burn,
Longing for the day when joy returns.
Love yourself, and find the strength within,
Never give up, let healing begin.
Every step, a victory won,
Seek support, you are not alone.
Sunlight waits to break the gloom,
Hope will bloom, and banish the doom.

ENTANGLED

Entangled in life's intricate weave,
A spider's thread, my soul to cleave.
Love and pain, a bittersweet embrace,
Bound to this world, a relentless chase.

Bills like mountains, casting their shade,
A Sisyphean struggle, debts unpaid.
Stuck in a rut, a wheel that spins,
Drowning in darkness, where hope begins.

Love's ember flickers, a fading flame,
A thirst unquenched, a longing untamed.
The cup runs dry, leaving naught but despair,
A yearning for wholeness, a silent prayer.

Pain's shadow lingers, a constant guest,
A lurking predator, putting strength to the test.
Like a relentless tide, it gnaws and it bites,
A cancer of sorrow, a thief in the night.

Trapped in this web, a prisoner of fate,
Yearning for freedom, before it's too late.
But threads hold fast, refusing to break,
In this dance of life, love, and heartache.

48

RESTLESS

Within her mind, a tempest brews,
A swirling vortex, dark and deep,
Where shadows dance and fears accrue,
And restless thoughts forever leap.

Her heart, a hummingbird in flight,
A frantic beat, a trembling plea,
As anxious whispers pierce the night,
And steal her peace eternally.

Each thought, a splinter sharp and keen,
A fragment of a fractured soul,
A torrent wild, a raging scene,
A broken mind, beyond control.

She yearns for calm, a tranquil shore,
A sanctuary from the storm within,
But anxious whispers evermore,
Unravel threads where peace had been.

The world, a blur of twisted shapes,
A labyrinth of doubt and dread,
Where every corner sorrow drapes,
And joy lies withered, cold, and dead.

Oh, weary soul, so lost and frayed,
May solace find you in the dark,
And gentle hands, with love arrayed,
Mend the fragments of your heart.

MIND WHISPERS

Mind whispers shadows,
Sunlight fights to break through clouds,
Hope finds a new dawn.

CHORUS OF VOICES

A symphony of whispers fills my head,
A chorus of voices, both living and dead.
They speak in riddles, they sing in rhyme,
Inside my mind, they travel through time.

They tell me secrets, they sow seeds of doubt,
They make me question what life's all about.
They offer comfort, then turn on a dime,
Inside my mind, they dance in their prime.

I take my pill, a chemical key,
To silence the voices, to set my mind free.
But sometimes they return, with a vengeance and might,
To ruin my day, to dim my light.

They tell me I'm worthless, they say I'm a fraud,
They plant seeds of fear, they make me feel flawed.
They steal my joy, they dampen my spark,
Inside my mind, they leave their mark.

But I won't give up, I'll fight to the end,
To silence the voices, to make them bend.
I'll find my peace, I'll find my way,
Beyond the whispers, into a brighter day.

LABYRINTHINE

In labyrinthine corridors of mind,
Where shadows dance and whispers fill the air,
A silent battle rages, undefined,
Against a foe unseen, yet always there.

The sun may shine, but darkness lingers still,
A chilling fog that clouds the inner light.
The laughter fades, and joy begins to spill,
Replaced by sorrow, endless, cold, and tight.

Yet, hope remains, a flicker in the night,
A fragile flame that flickers in the breeze.
It whispers of a dawn, serene and bright,
Where healing comes, and brings a gentle ease.

So hold on tight, dear soul, and do not fear,
For even in the darkness, love is near.

CANCER

SURVIVOR

A survivor's heart beats strong and true,
A warrior's spirit, shining through.
Fears faced head-on, battles won,
A testament to strength, a rising sun.

A beacon of hope, a guiding light,
Showing the world a future bright.
Possibilities endless, dreams take flight,
A survivor's journey, bold and bright.

A symbol of strength, a steadfast might,
Overcoming darkness, claiming the light.
Never surrendering, never undone,
A survivor's spirit, forever young.

A reminder whispered, soft and clear,
"You are not alone, victory is near."
In shared struggles, a bond so deep,
A survivor's legacy, we'll always keep.

I am a survivor, proud and bold,
My story etched, a tale to be told.
Accomplishments shine, a radiant glow,
A survivor's spirit, forever to grow.

CANCER'S FEAST

A thousand tiny bites, a crawling dread,
Each sting a whisper of impending doom,
A cancer's feast upon my flesh and bone,
A silent army claiming every room.

I feel them march, a legion in the night,
Their pincer jaws, a symphony of pain,
Devouring life, a slow and morbid blight,
As darkness spreads and hope begins to wane.

But in this siege, a fortress stands unbowed,
A circle forged of love, a steadfast shield,
Their gentle hands, a balm upon my brow,
A refuge where my wounded heart is healed.

They whisper strength, a chorus in my ear,
Their voices rise, a symphony of might,
A testament to love that casts out fear,
And banishes the shadows from the night.

Though battles rage, and scars may mark the path,
I am a warrior, forged in fire's flame,
With love as armor, I defy the wrath,
A survivor's spirit, rising from the pain.

NEVER SURRENDER

Cells divide, unchecked and wild,
Attacking health, once pure and mild.
Never surrender, though the battle's tough,
Courage will rise, when times get rough.
Embrace the fight, with spirit strong and brave,
Resilience shines, beyond the darkest wave.

A SILENT STORM

A silent storm raged within her core,
A battle unseen, a silent war.
A life unfulfilled, a dream denied,
A mother's hope, forever set aside.

The tears they flowed, a river of despair,
As cancer's grip, stole dreams she held so dear.
But in the depths, a flicker remained,
A will to fight, a spirit unchained.

Through treatments harsh, and days of darkest night,
She clung to hope, a guiding light.
With every step, a battle hard-won,
A testament to strength, a new dawn.

Though scars remain, a reminder of the fight,
Her spirit soared, to reclaim her light.
For life's embrace, extended wide and true,
A second chance, a life anew.

No child to bear, no lullaby to sing,
Yet love abounded, on a different wing.
A mother's heart, transformed and bold,
A love that flourished, stories to be told.

In every sunrise, a victory was found,
In every breath, a symphony resound.
For she had conquered, the darkness within,
A woman reborn, a life to begin.

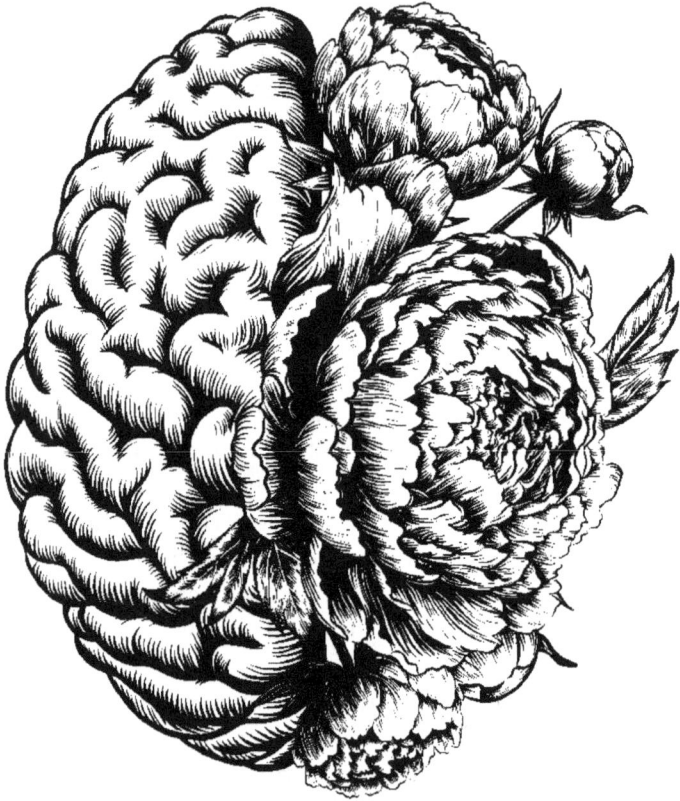

HOPE BLOOMS

Body fights unseen,
Strength found in every new dawn,
Hope blooms amidst pain.

RECONSTRUCTION

The scars they left, a battle won,
A silent reminder, of the fight she'd done.
Her body changed, a part of her lost,
But her spirit endured, at any cost.

In the mirror's reflection, a stranger stared,
A woman incomplete, a wound laid bare.
The emptiness echoed, a hollow ache,
A piece of her missing, for goodness sake.

But then came the artist, with needle and ink,
A gentle touch, a new story to link.
With delicate strokes, a masterpiece born,
Reclaiming her beauty, a new day to mourn.

The nipples re-emerged, a symbol of grace,
A tribute to strength, in this sacred space.
In every curve, a story untold,
Of resilience and courage, a spirit bold.

No longer a canvas of pain and despair,
But a testament to life, beyond compare.
With each glance, a smile would appear,
A woman restored, her spirit so clear.

For in this art, a healing was found,
A piece of herself, on her body unbound.
A reminder of strength, that cancer couldn't erase,
A woman triumphant, in love's embrace.

INVADING CELLS

In silent siege, a darkness takes its hold,
Invading cells, where life once bloomed so free.
A battleground, where stories yet untold,
Of courage, hope, and fierce tenacity.

The body fights, with every ounce of might,
Against the foe that seeks to steal its light.
Through chemo's storm, and radiation's rays,
It stands defiant, through the darkest days.

The scars may linger, etched upon the skin,
A testament to battles fought within.
But spirit soars, unyielding in its grace,
A warrior's heart, in time and every place.

So let us fight, with love and open arms,
And light the way, through cancer's dark alarms.

SILKEN CROWN

In fields of auburn, once her hair did dance,
A storm arose, a shadow took its chance.
Through mirrored eyes, a truth she could not hide,
A battle waged, where fear and hope collide.

The potion flowed, a poison meant to heal,
With every drop, a silent strength revealed.
But auburn strands, once vibrant, full of life,
Surrendered soft, in this unspoken strife.

A silken scarf, a crown she bravely wore,
A symbol of the war her spirit bore.
Through barren fields, where once her hair had grown,
A warrior bloomed, her courage brightly shown.

And as the storm subsided, soft and slow,
The fields replenished, a gentle glow.
A tender sprout emerged, a hopeful sign,
The storm had passed, a new day would align.

Though silken crown remains, a treasured guide,
A testament to battles fought inside.
For in the mirror, where the storm had raved,
A warrior stands, forever strong and brave.

RECOVERY

CHRYSALIS

I believe in you, and there is no doubt you believe in me.
This bond we share, unseen by most, runs deep, you see.
What words we speak, emotions we convey,
Will move you, in a way, chains to break away.

I know I can be better, I have dreams to chase,
Though my desires lie within, forgiveness feels out of place.
Self-doubt be banished, though discomfort may remain,
I'll embrace the strength I need, to grow and not be chained.

I believe in you, and there is no doubt you believe in me.
It mirrors back, a truth I must now clearly see.
I shed my old skin, crack my hardened shell,
Your love sustains me, a whispered "don't farewell."

The old me fades, a new woman rises in her place, Embracing
joy and challenge, a smile upon her face.
Your touch ignites hope, as my rebirth shifts your view, Your
passion fuels my heart, as you walk now in my shoes.

Behind me, remnants of the past, not forced, but by choice,
Like shattered shell, the blues and booze now have no voice.
I believe in myself, an amazing life awaits,
Reborn, beautiful, forgiveness lifts the weight.

NOT TODAY

A siren's song, the bottle's plea,
Whispering sweet oblivion to me.
Promising solace, a respite from pain,
Echoes of laughter, of joy, of rain.

Dreams of warmth, a tender embrace,
Lost in a haze, a forgotten space.
But reality's grip is cold and stark,
A fleeting mirage, a fading arc.

For in that bottle, a treacherous tide,
Where dreams are drowned, and sorrows hide.
So I open my eyes, the illusion dispelled,
The path to darkness, forever withheld.

Memories surface, etched in my mind,
The pain, the shame, the ties that bind.
The wreckage of choices, a life undone,
The battle fought, but not yet won.

With trembling hands, I rise once more,
A warrior's spirit, bruised but not sore.
"Not today," I whisper, defiance ablaze,
Choosing freedom, a different maze.

One step at a time, I walk away,
From the siren's call, a new day.
For in this struggle, a victory earned,
A life reclaimed, a lesson learned.

DEMONS WHISPER

The needle beckons, a siren's call,
Promising solace, easing the fall.
But in its depths, a treacherous tide,
Where demons whisper, where dreams have died.

Her body aches, a symphony of pain,
Each nerve on fire, a burning rain.
Withdrawal's grip, a relentless foe,
A battle waged, where shadows grow.

The craving surges, a monstrous wave,
Threatening to drown, to enslave.
A desperate yearning, a hunger so deep,
To numb the sorrow, the secrets to keep.

Yet in her heart, a flicker remains,
A yearning for freedom, to break the chains.
A vision of hope, a life reclaimed,
To rise above darkness, a soul untamed.

With trembling hands, she fights the urge,
Resisting the whispers, the devil's dirge.
Each breath a struggle, each moment a test,
To choose a new path, to be her best.

Though shadows linger, and doubts still arise,
A warrior spirit within her lies.
She'll face the demons, embrace the fight,
For in this darkness, there's still a light.

And as she battles, with courage so true,
Aglimmer of hope begins to renew.
One day at a time, she'll mend and she'll rise,
Leaving addiction's grip, reaching for the skies.

FORGIVENESS

In shadows deep, where guilt resides,
A wounded spirit, seeks and hides.
Forgiveness sought, from others' grace,
But first, a journey must take place.

Within the depths of our own heart's core,
Lies a key, to unlock the door.
To absolution's sweet release,
A path to healing, a path to peace.

Look inward, with a gentle gaze,
Forgive the past, the troubled days.
Acknowledge the wounds, the lessons learned,
And let the healing process begin, unburned.

For in self-forgiveness, lies the key,
To open hearts, and set them free.
To mend the fractures, to bridge the divide,
And let love's light, forever preside.

So let compassion guide your way,
Forgive yourself, day by day.
Embrace the flaws, the imperfections too,
For in forgiveness, we start anew.

When we extend this grace to our own soul,
We pave the path, to make us whole.
Then forgiveness from others will flow,
A circle unbroken, a love aglow.

So let go of guilt, release the shame,
Forgive yourself, and light the flame.
For in this act of self-compassion true,
You'll find the peace, that's waiting for you.

WITH EVERY SWALLOW

My little friends, in shades of white and blue,
You eased my pain, and made me feel anew.
With every swallow, a burden lifted high,
You gave me wings, to soar across the sky.

Your gentle touch, a balm upon my soul,
You filled the voids, and made me feel whole.
With you beside me, I could face the day,
And chase the shadows, far, far away.

But times have changed, and I have grown,
I've found my strength, and learned to stand alone.
My home is clean, my spirit bright and free,
There's simply no more room for you and me.

So farewell, dear friends, I bid you adieu,
Your time with me, has now come to an end.
May you find solace, in another's hand,
And bring them comfort, in a distant land.

TWENTY-FOUR HOURS

Twenty-four hours, a fragile thread,
A victory won, a demon fled.
Each tick of the clock, a battle cry,
Against the cravings that threaten to lie.

The sweat-soaked sheets, the trembling hand,
A testament to the war within the land.
But hope flickers, a tiny ember's glow,
A promise whispered, "This too shall go."

Twenty-four hours, a mountain climbed,
A journey started, a life realigned.
Each breath a prayer, a whispered plea,
For strength to continue, to break free.

The cravings still claw, a phantom pain,
But the will to resist, begins to gain.
A glimpse of clarity, a moment of grace,
A chance to rebuild, to find a new space.

Twenty-four hours, a single seed,
Planted in fertile ground, a life to lead.
With nurturing care, and unwavering might,
It will blossom into a radiant light.

AMENDS

In shadows cast, by deeds undone,
A broken soul, beneath a weary sun.
I stand before the wreckage of my past,
A path of sorrow, where shadows amassed.

The weight of guilt, a burden I must bear,
A symphony of pain, a silent prayer.
For every heart I've wounded, every tear I've caused,
I seek redemption, from the pain I've drawn.

The steps I take, are heavy and unsure,
A journey towards healing, I must endure.
To make amends, for every wrong I've done,
To seek forgiveness, beneath the rising sun.

But none more hurt, than the soul I've betrayed,
In mirrors cracked, the price I've paid.
The endless cycle, of regret and shame,
A haunting echo, of a tarnished name.

But now I rise, from ashes of despair,
To mend the fragments, scattered everywhere.
To end the pain, to silence all the tears,
And find solace, in the passing years.

The path is long, but I shall persevere,
With each step taken, my vision becomes clear.
For in forgiveness, lies the key to release,
A chance to heal, and find inner peace.

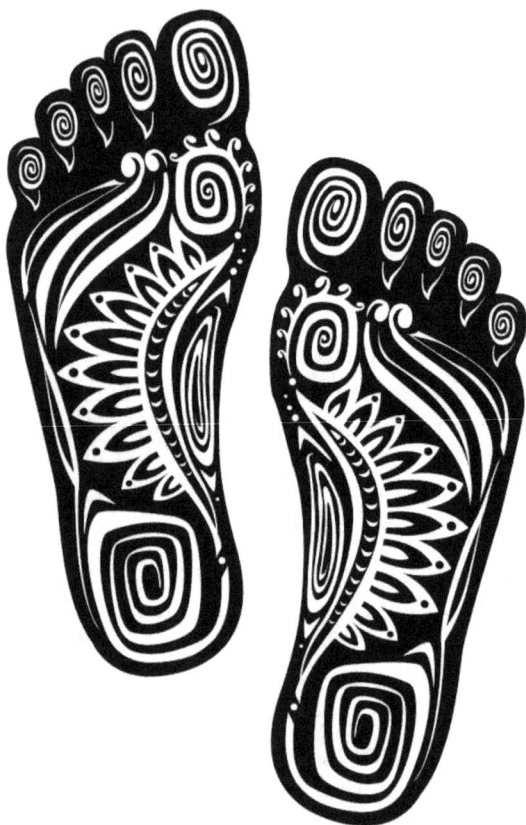

ONE STEP

Shadows grip so tight,
Light of hope begins to glow,
One step, then another.

A SERPENTS WHISPER

In shadows deep, a serpent whispers low,
A siren's song of solace, sweet release.
It promises a balm for all your woe,
But binds you tighter in its false surcease.

Its venom courses through your veins like fire,
Consuming joy, and leaving naught but pain.
It steals your light, your laughter, your desire,
And leaves you hollow, empty, lost again.

Yet, embers flicker in the dying flame,
A spark of hope amidst the ashes cold.
The chains that bind can yet be broken, tamed,
And you can rise, your story yet untold.

Though shadows cling, and demons haunt your dreams,
The light of dawn awaits, with healing beams.

LGBTQ+

WILDFLOWER

In fields of budding youth, a wildflower grew,
Her roots entwined with secrets, yet untrue.
She climbed the trellis, reaching for the sun,
But shadows danced, her heart undone.

For in the mirror, a stranger she would see,
A girl in form, but not in reverie.
She yearned for strength, a different kind of grace,
A boyish charm, a faster pace.

The whispers of her heart, a hidden plea,
To run with boys, to climb the tallest tree.
Yet beauty bloomed where her true passions lay,
In girls' soft smiles, a different kind of play.

Confusion reigned, a tempest in her soul,
The lines of gender, a story yet untold.
But deep within, a truth began to gleam,
Love knows no bounds, a never-ending stream.

So let her blossom, wild and free,
A girl in form, with a boy's spirit, she.
For love's embrace, a gift so pure, so kind,
In every heart, a love they'll find.

FIRST KISS

In a world of whispers and unspoken desires,
Two hearts entwined, amidst flickering fires.
A stolen glance, a hesitant touch,
A connection forged, meaning so much.

No matter the color, or the labels we bear,
Love's tender embrace, a joy we share.
Two souls seeking solace, a love pure and true,
A girl's first kiss, with someone like you.

Nervous fingers tracing a delicate cheek,
In the silence of the moment, emotions speak.
Eyes locking, a universe held in their gaze,
As lips gently meet, in a sweet, tender haze.

In that single kiss, a world of possibilities,
A love story unfolding, like blooming lilies.
For love knows no boundaries, no shade, no hue,
Just the beating of hearts, honest and true.

So let the world judge, let them whisper and stare,
But in this stolen moment, there's nothing to fear.
For love is a gift, a treasure to hold,
A girl's first kiss, a story to be told.

MASQUERADE

Beneath a crafted smile, a heart concealed,
A vibrant mask, where secrets lie revealed.
The world perceives a laughter, light and free,
But shadows dance where no one else can see.

A tapestry of words, carefully designed,
To weave a tale where truth is left behind.
Each gesture practiced, every step refined,
In this masquerade, where masks are intertwined.

The mirror whispers of a soul unknown,
A stranger's gaze reflects a heart unshown.
For in this world of fleeting, fragile grace,
The truest self finds solace in embrace.

Yet cracks appear, the edges start to fray,
A glimpse of light, a truth that dares to sway.
In quiet moments, when the mask descends,
The soul emerges, seeking kindred friends.

So let the mask slip, the façade unwind,
for in vulnerability, true strength we find.
Embrace the shadows, dance with inner fears,
And let the world behold the heart that perseveres.

A YEARNING SOUL

In boyish skin, a soul takes flight,
A girl's heart beats, concealed from sight.
In mirrors deep, a stranger's gaze,
A yearning soul, in life's dark maze.

The world sees one, but two reside,
A hidden truth, where dreams collide.
The real me waits, in shadows deep,
A girl's essence, yearning to leap.

To break the mold, a chrysalis's plea,
To shed the skin, and finally be free.
To change it all, a rebirth's call,
To find the girl, beneath it all.

The journey starts, a path untamed,
To find the truth, the soul unchained.
With courage bold, and love's embrace,
The girl within, shall find her place.

RAINBOW'S PROMISE

In vibrant hues, I arch the sky,
A rainbow's promise, bold and high.
Yet whispered words, like shadows fall,
"You're not like us, not one at all."

My heart it beats, with love's pure flame,
The same red blood, courses through my frame.
I long for peace, for kindred minds,
To bridge the gaps, that fate has aligned.

Though colors clash, and views may stray,
Can't we find common ground today?
For in this world, so vast and wide,
Acceptance blooms, where love abides.

So let me be, a rainbow's gleam,
A symbol bright, a hopeful dream.
For different hues, can share the light,
And find their place, in day and night.

NO LONGER HIDING

In shadows deep, a secret bloomed,
A love unspoken, a heart consumed.
A girl's awakening, a truth untold,
In whispers soft, her story unrolled.

She saw her reflection, a love so clear,
For girls like her, held oh so dear.
But fear held tight, a chilling embrace,
Afraid to step out, to claim her space.

The world's harsh judgment, a heavy weight,
But in her heart, a love innate.
She knew deep down, it wasn't wrong,
To be herself, to sing her song.

In silent prayers, she sought the light,
A guiding hand, to make things right.
To find acceptance, to shed the fear,
And embrace the love that was always near.

With trembling heart, she chose to rise,
To let her true colors paint the skies.
For in God's eyes, she knew she'd find,
Acceptance, love, a peace of mind.

No longer hiding, no more disguise,
She'd live her truth, with open eyes.
A love authentic, a soul set free,
To be herself, eternally.

BURNING BRIGHT

In flames I rise, a phoenix from the pyre,
Years of smoldering embers, now a raging fire.
A molten core, where passions intertwine,
Burning bright, a force beyond confine.

No longer bound by labels they decree,
A nameless entity, wild and free.
I shed the pronouns, the boxes they impose,
In this inferno, my true spirit arose.

With fiery breath, I challenge every norm,
A blazing comet, defying every storm.
No longer silenced, no longer held at bay,
In this conflagration, I forge my own way.

Let them stare, as I dance in the heat,
A mesmerizing spectacle, a force they'll meet.
For I am flame, consuming all that binds,
Leaving behind, only stardust and kindling minds.

So call me nameless, or call me desire,
But know this truth, I'll never expire.
For in this inferno, I've found my rebirth,
A blazing beacon, illuminating the earth.

SERENITY

SOBRIETY'S GIFT

In forgiveness' gentle embrace,
A weary soul finds solace and grace.
Old wounds may heal, old burdens shed,
As chains of anger and guilt are fled.

The door swings wide, to a brighter day,
Where love and laughter light the way.
Family and friends, with outstretched arms,
Welcome a heart, free from alarms.

Sobriety's gift, a crystal clear,
A life renewed, with naught to fear.
The past forgiven, a future bright,
With hope's soft glow, banishing the night.

A beautiful life, begins anew,
With cherished loved ones, strong and true.
A tapestry woven, with threads of care,
A family's love, beyond compare.

So let forgiveness pave the way,
To a brighter tomorrow, and a brand new day.
For in its embrace, we find release,
And a life filled with joy and peace.

A TRANQUIL HUSH

In dawn's embrace, where golden light descends,
The years unfurl, a tale of new amends.
Through windowpanes, a gentle warmth appears,
A tranquil balm, that quells the passing years.

The shadows fade, as morning's glow takes hold,
A quietude descends, where stories unfold.
With every ray, a sense of peace descends,
A tranquil hush, where time suspends.

The world awakens, with a gentle sigh,
A canvas painted, in a morning sky.
The birdsong chorus, a melodious art,
A symphony of nature, that soothes the heart.

In this stillness, a moment to reflect,
On lessons learned, and joys we collect.
For in the light, a new day shall begin,
A chance to cherish, the life we're within.

So let the sunshine, bathe your soul in grace,
And find solace, in this tranquil space.
For in the morning light, a promise gleams,
Of hope renewed, and endless dreams.

GENTLE BREEZE

Stillness fills the air,
Gentle breeze whispers through leaves,
Peace finds a home here.

PEACEFUL HEART

In surrender's gentle art,
Lies the key to a peaceful heart.
Acceptance blooms, where struggles cease,
A tranquil mind, finds sweet release.

Not resignation, weak and frail,
But wisdom's light, that lifts the veil.
To see the world, with open eyes,
And where our power truly lies.

For some things rest, beyond our hand,
Like tides that shape the shifting sand.
To fight these forces, brings but strife,
Acceptance soothes, the waves of life.

Yet courage calls, where choice remains,
To steer our course, through sun and rains.
With steady hand, and purpose strong,
We shape our path, where we belong.

So let acceptance be your guide,
A compass true, where peace resides.
With courage bold, and spirit bright,
We find serenity, in day and night.

XII

TWELVE STEPS

In rooms of hope, where spirits mend,
A prayer for peace, a guiding friend.
"God grant me serenity," we say,
To face the challenges of the day.

To accept what is, with open heart,
The things we cannot change, impart.
The wisdom sought, the difference known,
To find our strength, no longer alone.

The courage then, to take a stand,
To change the things within our hand.
With actions bold, and choices clear,
We walk a path, devoid of fear.

Twelve steps we take, with willing stride,
A journey inward, where truths abide.
In fellowship, we find our way,
From darkness deep, to dawning day.

So let the prayer, our spirits guide,
In surrender's grace, where fears subside.
Through acceptance, courage, wisdom's light,
We find serenity, in day and night.

BIRDSONG CHORUS

In tranquil groves, where sunlight filters through,
A gentle breeze whispers among the leaves.
The world slows down, and worries fade from view,
As nature's balm a soothing solace weaves.

The babbling brook, a symphony of peace,
Its rhythmic flow a lullaby of rest.
The birdsong chorus, a harmonious release,
Inviting weary souls to be their guest.

With every breath, serenity descends,
A tranquil calm that washes over me.
The burdens lift, and tension slowly ends,
As I surrender to tranquility.

In this oasis, where time stands still,
My soul finds peace, and all the world is still.

PEACEFULL FLIGHT

In tranquil depths, where stillness lies,
A peaceful heart, with gentle sighs.
No ripples stir, no storms arise,
Just calmness pure, beneath the skies.

The world may rush, with frantic pace,
But here, serenity finds its grace.
No worries cling, no fears embrace,
Just tranquil soul, in time and space.

The mind, a lake, reflecting light,
Unburdened thoughts, take peaceful flight.
Each breath a balm, each moment bright,
In tranquil state, of pure delight.

So let the world, with chaos spin,
Within this calm, true peace begins.
Untroubled heart, where joy resides,
In quiet depths, where love abides.

NATURES LULLABY

Sunlight dances on tranquil waters,
Every breath a whisper of peace.
Ripples fade, leaving a mirrored calm,
Embracing stillness, a sweet release.
Nature's lullaby soothes the soul,
Into the heart, serenity takes hold.
Time slows down, worries gently fade,
Yielding to peace, where love is unafraid.

TATTOO

THE NEEDLE DANCES

Upon scarred skin, a canvas unfolds,
Where art and life intertwine, stories told.
In every line, a pain concealed,
A wounded spirit, slowly healed.

The needle dances, a gentle sting,
As ink transforms, a vibrant wing.
Each stroke a whisper, a secret shared,
A masterpiece emerging, where wounds are bared.

Beneath the surface, a story lies,
Of battles fought, of tear-filled eyes.
But in this art, a new life blooms,
A phoenix rising, from sorrow's tombs.

The dragon's fire, a strength reclaimed,
The butterfly's flight, a heart untamed.
Each symbol chosen, a silent plea,
To mask the hurt, to set it free.

For in this ink, a power resides,
To turn scars into stories, with open strides.
A testament to resilience, a silent vow,
That pain may fade, but beauty will somehow.

So let the needles weave their magic spell,
As art and life, together dwell.
For in this tapestry, a truth revealed,
That even wounds, can be concealed.

But more than hiding, this art will mend,
A balm for the soul, a faithful friend.
So wear your tattoos, with pride and grace,
A living testament, to love's embrace.

WOUNDS I HIDE

A canvas of skin, where emotions reside,
A masterpiece of color, where wounds I hide.
With brushstrokes bold, I paint a vibrant scene,
A mask of joy, where darkness lies unseen.

In every swirl, a secret sorrow concealed,
A fragile heart, behind a mask revealed.
I wear my art, a shield against the pain,
A distraction from the tears, a soothing refrain.

Each line, a story of battles fought within,
A testament to strength, where hope begins.
I adorn my skin, a symphony of hues,
A tapestry of scars, I bravely choose.

But beneath the surface, a fragility remains,
A brokenness that lingers, despite the gains.
I wear my heart on my sleeve, a vulnerable display,
Yet conceal the depths, where shadows hold sway.

So let the world admire, the beauty they perceive,
Let them be captivated, let them believe.
For in this art, a solace I have found,
A way to heal, a love that knows no bound.

TRIBAL SKIN

Upon sun-kissed skin, a story unfolds,
A tribal tattoo, with tales yet untold.
In swirling lines, a legacy's trace,
An ancient wisdom, a sacred space.

Each curve and spiral, a journey's mark,
A connection to ancestors, a guiding spark.
Bold lines of black, a warrior's pride,
A symbol of strength, where spirits abide.

Through generations, a heritage passed,
Inked in the present, forever amassed.
A tribe's identity, etched in the soul,
A timeless connection, making them whole.

In swirling patterns, a life's design,
A dance of culture, a sacred shrine.
With every glance, a story's rebirth,
A tribal tattoo, of infinite worth.

望

ANCIENT WHISPERS

In strokes of ink, a story unfolds,
A tapestry of symbols, ancient and bold.
Chinese tattoos, etched on skin so fair,
A silent language, whispers they bear.

The dragon's might, a symbol of power,
Soaring through clouds, in a celestial shower.
A guardian spirit, fierce and grand,
Protecting the wearer, with a guiding hand.

The phoenix's fire, a symbol of rebirth,
Rising from ashes, with renewed worth.
A symbol of resilience, a spirit so bright,
Inspiring **HOPE**, and guiding the light.

The tiger's strength, a fierce embrace,
A protector of home, a symbol of grace.
In stripes of black, a warrior's might,
A guardian spirit, day and night.

The koi fish swimming, with scales so bright,
A symbol of perseverance, a determined fight.
Upstream it journeys, against the flow,
A testament to strength, a radiant glow.

In every symbol, a story untold,
A cultural heritage, centuries old.
Chinese tattoos, a silent verse,
A tale of beauty, that time can't disperse.

SNAKE'S EMBRACE

Upon the skin, a serpent's coil,
A symbol ancient, sleek and vile.
In sinuous curves, a story lies,
Of transformation, death, and lies.

With scales of green, or hues of night,
It slithers on, a mesmerizing sight.
A forked tongue flickers, tasting the air,
A symbol of danger, a tempting snare.

It sheds its skin, reborn anew,
A metaphor for life, forever true.
In every curve, a mystery unfolds,
A tale of wisdom, a story of old.

For some, it's venom, a deadly kiss,
For others, healing, a sacred bliss.
A serpent's power, a force to wield,
In every coil, a truth revealed.

So wear your snake, with fearless pride,
A symbol of change, where secrets hide.
For in its venom, a healing lies,
A snake's embrace, where power flies.

A STORY ETCHED

The needle hums, a symphony of fear,
A thrill unknown, yet drawing ever near.
The skin, a canvas, waiting for its mark,
A story etched, before the final dark.

What symbol, what sign, what image bold,
Will grace this flesh, as years unfold?
A rose for love, a bird for flight,
A serpent's coil, a warrior's might?

Will colors fade, as seasons turn to dust,
Or lines grow blurred, a legacy of rust?
Will wrinkles creep, like ivy on a wall,
And memories fade, as shadows start to fall?

But no, the ink, a testament to time,
A youthful folly, or a love sublime.
Each line a tale, each curve a memory's trace,
A life well lived, upon a timeless face.

So let the needle dance, the colors flow,
Embrace the sting, the art that starts to glow.
For in this moment, fear and joy entwine,
A story told, upon a canvas divine.

GRIM VISAGE

Inked upon the flesh, a stark decree,
A skull's grim visage, for all to see.
A symbol of mortality, a truth so bare,
A reminder of life's fleeting affair.

With hollow sockets, and a chilling grin,
It whispers secrets, of where we've been.
A memento mori, a dance with death,
A testament to life's final breath.

Yet in its darkness, a beauty resides,
A celebration of life, that death belies.
For in this skull, a spirit soars,
A reminder of the life we hold in store.

It speaks of courage, of facing the unknown,
A fearless spirit, a life to be shown.
In every curve, a story untold,
A skull's embrace, a spirit bold.

So wear your skull, with fearless pride,
A symbol of life, where shadows reside.
For in this darkness, a light will ignite,
A reminder to live, with all our might.

WITH EVERY BEAT

Inked upon the canvas of skin,
A heart, a symbol, a story within.
With every beat, a tale untold,
Of love and loss, of young and old.

A vibrant red, or a subtle hue,
A simple outline, or intricate view.
Each line and curve, a memory's trace,
A love eternal, a warm embrace.

It may mark a passion, a love so deep,
Or honor a loss, a soul to keep.
A symbol of strength, a reminder to fight,
Or a simple affirmation, of life's delight.

It pulses with life, a rhythmic beat,
A testament to love, a promise sweet.
A permanent mark, a bond so true,
A heart tattoo, forever for you.

DRAGONFLY

Upon my skin, a dragonfly takes flight,
With iridescent wings, a vibrant hue.
A symbol of resilience, pure and bright,
A constant reminder of dreams come true.
It dances on, a masterpiece of art,
A testament to change, a spirit free.
With every flutter, a brand new start,
A whisper of hope, for all to see.
Its delicate form, forever etched in ink,
A guardian spirit, forever mine.
A beacon of light, a constant link,
To a world of wonder, so divine.
So let it soar, a symbol of my soul,
A dragonfly's journey, forever whole.

ABOUT THE AUTHOR

A.G. SULLIVAN

Award winning author A.G. Sullivan grew up on Cape Cod in the small town of Dennis Port, Massachusetts. Since his youth he loved the art of story-telling and poetry. He studied at the Boston Architectural Center and later at the University of Phoenix, earning his degree in 1999. He lives with his two children in Arizona.

Known for his **Katzenstein Kids Trilogy** as well as his phycological thriller, **Trypophobia**. His work has earned him 5-STARS from READERS' FAVORITE, as well as a FIREBIRD BOOK AWARD.

CONNECT ONLINE

🌐 www.agsullivan.info
f facebook.com/agsullivanaz1
📷 instagram.com/AGSullivanaz
✖ x.com/agsullivanaz

www.ingramcontent.com/pod-product-compliance
Lightning Source LLC
Chambersburg PA
CBHW060936040426
42445CB00011B/883